Moving Beyond The

MYTHS

STUDY GUIDE

MYTHS

STUDY GUIDE

HOPE AND ENCOURAGEMENT FOR WOMEN

JAN SILVIOUS

MOODY PRESS
CHICAGO

All Scripture quotations, unless otherwise indicated, are taken from the *New American Stan-
dard Bible*®, © Copyright The Lockman Foundation 1960, 1962, 1963, 1968, 1971, 1972,
1973, 1975, 1977, 1995. Used by permission.

ISBN: 0-8024-6585-4

1 3 5 7 9 10 8 6 4 2

Printed in the United States of America

CONTENTS

ACKNOWLEDGMENT

Many thanks to Joye Howard for her work on this Study Guide.

INTRODUCTION

As you read through the book *Moving Beyond the Myths: Hope and Encouragement for Women,* you will be faced with many myths you believed in the past and possibly continue to believe. The only way to destroy a myth is to replace it with truth. However, it is easy to read a truth, agree with it mentally, but remain unchanged.

The purpose of this companion guide is to help you apply the truth to your life in a very real way. As you complete each chapter in the book, turn to the corresponding chapter in this Study Guide. As you read the questions, pause after each one and ask the Lord to reveal areas that He wants to change in you. Don't be overly introspective, but be willing to allow Him to show you the truth about your thinking. If you are open to hear from Him, He will speak to you.

Make a commitment to record the things the Lord shows you as a result of reading the questions—and especially the Scriptures. Writing down your thoughts will help you think more clearly. If you find that you need more room to write than is provided in this book, get a small notebook and start a journal. This can be a very useful tool to review the ways God has worked in your life and relationships.

CHAPTER ONE
MISERABLE MYTHS

As you read chapter 1, did you find yourself exclaiming, "That's me!" "I thought I was the only one living in defeat." "That is exactly the frustration and despair I am feeling."

Did your heart cry out, "I want to experience that peace and contentment." "I want to know the truth!"

Or maybe you were a little apprehensive at the thought of questioning the things you have always heard. Maybe you have questioned before and have been reproved for rocking the boat.

If you are going to challenge your belief system, you may find it uncomfortable and maybe frightening. There will be those who will come against you and cause you to waver. There will be times when discouragement takes over and you wonder if it is worth it. There will be times when the only thing you can do is to cling to God and His promises.

A trend in recent years is to humanize God, to limit His power to what we are capable of humanly understanding. Therefore, in order to abandon yourself totally to God, it is urgent that you understand who God is and His power and faithfulness. Read the following Scriptures and ask God to reveal Himself to you. As He speaks to your heart, record what you learn about Him. Writing down the truths God reveals about Himself will help clarify your thinking and seal them to your heart.

Psalm 18:30–36
As for God, His way is blameless;
The word of the Lord is tried;
He is a shield to all who take refuge in Him.
For who is God, but the Lord?
And who is a rock, except our God,
The God who girds me with strength
And makes my way blameless?
He makes my feet like hinds' feet,
And sets me upon my high places.
He trains my hands for battle,
So that my arms can bend a bow of bronze.
You have also given me the shield of Your salvation,
And Your right hand upholds me;
And Your gentleness makes me great.
You enlarge my steps under me,
And my feet have not slipped.

Psalm 19:7–10
The law of the Lord is perfect, restoring the soul;
The testimony of the Lord is sure, making wise the simple.
The precepts of the Lord are right, rejoicing the heart;
The commandment of the Lord is pure, enlightening the eyes.
The fear of the Lord is clean, enduring forever;
The judgments of the Lord are true; they are righteous altogether.
They are more desirable than gold, yes, than much fine gold;
Sweeter also than honey and the drippings of the honeycomb.

Can God be trusted? Can you trust Him as you question those things you have heard and believed for many years? If your desire is to abandon yourself to God and trust Him to examine the things you believe and reveal truth, why not take a moment to write out your prayer of commitment. God knows your heart, but writing it seals it to *your* heart.

As you challenge your belief system, there will be times of frustration, times of discouragement, times of defeat, times of depression. As a result, your thinking may become muddled, you may not understand, you may wonder why. At those times return to the Scriptures you have just studied, read the truths that God revealed to you—and believe them. Regardless of how you feel, by an act of your will, say, "I don't feel this but I choose to believe it anyway." The most important truth to hang on to is that *God is who He says He is, and He will do what He says He will do.*

CHAPTER TWO

MYTHS IN THE GARDEN

What is in your life that God just can't handle? What have you prayed about over and over, but nothing seems to happen and God just doesn't respond? Take a minute to note that concern. You don't have to spell it out. You can use your own form of shorthand so you can keep your thoughts private, if you wish.

Why didn't God intervene when I (my child, my relative, my friend) was being abused? Why didn't He stop that devastating illness? Why has He not answered when I prayed about the matter I recorded? God just doesn't care or He would fix things. Maybe there is something wrong with *me*. Maybe I'm not good enough. I just don't understand.

Maybe you have hit on something here. *You just don't understand.*

We don't understand God and His ways. We have molded God into our own image. We are trying to get Him to meet our agenda, and when He doesn't, we feel that He is holding out on us.

God longs for a trusting relationship with His children. In order to trust Him, we must know His character and His ways. As you explore what God says, why not make a note so that you can read these pages again and remember.

What are God's thoughts toward you?

Jeremiah 31:3
"I have loved you with an everlasting love;
Therefore I have drawn you with lovingkindness."

Is He holding out on you?

Deuteronomy 7:9
"Know therefore that the Lord your God, He is God, the faithful God, who

keeps His covenant and His lovingkindness to a thousandth generation with
those who love Him and keep His commandments."

Can you really trust Him?

Lamentations 3:21–24
This I recall to my mind,
Therefore I have hope.
The Lord's lovingkindnesses indeed never cease,
For His compassions never fail.
They are new every morning;
Great is Your faithfulness.
"The Lord is my portion," says my soul,
"Therefore I have hope in Him."

But why? Why did God allow . . .

Proverbs 3:5–8
Trust in the Lord with all your heart
And do not lean on your own understanding.
In all your ways acknowledge Him,
And He will make your paths straight.
Do not be wise in your own eyes;
Fear the Lord and turn away from evil.
It will be healing to your body
And refreshment to your bones.

Be honest with God. Tell Him about your frustrations and the times you felt He was holding out on you. Then review the Scriptures you have just read, putting in your own name and allowing God to touch your heart with His lovingkindness. Trust Him with your deepest concerns. He loves you. He really does.

CHAPTER THREE

THE MYTH
OF
DAMAGED GOODS

I s there something in your past that keeps haunting you, telling you that you are not good enough? What is it? Again, use your own form of shorthand for privacy.

Are you trying to please someone or prove to them that you are of value? Who?

Is there something about your physical body that you feel makes you unacceptable? What?

Do you constantly put yourself down, perhaps secretly hoping someone will contradict you?

Do you feel dependent upon approval of others for your sense of self-worth? Do you make your decisions and form your actions based upon whether they will please or displease someone?

Have you been caught up in damaging relationships in an effort to get approval?

Who does God say you are? What value does God place upon you as His child?

Ephesians 2:10
For we are His workmanship, created in Christ Jesus for good works, which God prepared beforehand so that we would walk in them.

Romans 8:16–17
The Spirit Himself testifies with our spirit that we are children of God, and if children, heirs also, heirs of God and fellow heirs with Christ, if indeed we suffer with Him so that we may also be glorified with Him.

1 Corinthians 3:16–17
Do you not know that you are a temple of God and that the Spirit of God dwells in you? If any man destroys the temple of God, God will destroy him, for the temple of God is holy, and that is what you are.

2 Corinthians 5:17
Therefore if anyone is in Christ, he is a new creature; the old things passed away; behold, new things have come.

Psalm 139:13–14
For You formed my inward parts;
You wove me in my mother's womb.
I will give thanks to You, for I am fearfully and wonderfully made;
Wonderful are Your works,
And my soul knows it very well.

This is God's evaluation of you, His child. Can you believe it? Spend some real time meditating on these truths. Look at your past through the light of these truths. View your physical body through the mirror of these truths. Judge your value as a person on the foundation of these truths. It takes time for this to become a habit, but you can begin right now.

CHAPTER FOUR

THE MYTH
OF
RESPONSIBILITY

Who or what is the crowd in your life? Make a list of the things that are crowding your mind and your life, the things you feel responsible for, the things that are stealing the time you should be spending on the important things. You may have a list of people. Your shorthand would be a good idea as you identify your crowd.

As you review each item on the list, ask yourself the questions that were posed in chapter 4 of *Moving Beyond the Myths: Hope and Encouragement for Women.*

Who is in control?

Daniel 2:20–22
Daniel said,
"Let the name of God be blessed forever and ever,
For wisdom and power belong to Him.
It is He who changes the times and the epochs;
He removes kings and establishes kings;
He gives wisdom to wise men
And knowledge to men of understanding.
It is He who reveals the profound and hidden things;
He knows what is in the darkness,
And the light dwells with Him."

Who will take care of you?

Psalm 94:14
For the Lord will not abandon His people,
Nor will He forsake His inheritance.

Does God know your need?

Psalm 139:1–5
O Lord, You have searched me and known me.
You know when I sit down and when I rise up;
You understand my thought from afar.
You scrutinize my path and my lying down,
And are intimately acquainted with all my ways.
Even before there is a word on my tongue,
Behold, O Lord, You know it all.
You have enclosed me behind and before,
And laid Your hand upon me."

What can you do about tomorrow?

Proverbs 27:1
Do not boast about tomorrow,
For you do not know what a day may bring forth.

The time has come to commit your crowd to the Lord. You may be able to release all of them at once. Or you may have to deal with them one at a time. The important thing is to start—now!

Psalm 55:22
Cast your burden upon the Lord and He will sustain you;
He will never allow the righteous to be shaken.

2 Timothy 2:4
No soldier in active service entangles himself in the affairs of everyday life, so that he may please the one who enlisted him as a soldier.

Jeremiah 17:7–8
"Blessed is the man who trusts in the Lord
And whose trust is the Lord.
For he will be like a tree planted by the water,
That extends its roots by a stream
And will not fear when the heat comes;
But its leaves will be green,
And it will not be anxious in a year of drought
Nor cease to yield fruit."

CHAPTER FIVE

THE MYTH
OF MARRIAGE
IS THE ANSWER

He was your knight in shining armor, your dream come true. He was going to meet your every need. He was going to make you complete.

But the armor has tarnished, the dream has faded. Why? Because he could not meet your needs and you are anything but complete. Another myth has failed to live up to its claims.

Is this your story? Is this where you are?

Or are you still living in the first half of the story protesting, "No, that is not going to happen to me. We are different."

Or maybe you are still living in the first half of the story and becoming more frustrated because there doesn't seem to be anyone to make you complete. Maybe your story has never started.

Regardless of where you are, the end does not have to be unhappy. This myth, like all others, must be replaced with truth. The death-blow to this myth will come when you realize who and what makes you complete.

Colossians 2:9–10
For in Him all the fullness of Deity dwells in bodily form, and in Him you have been made complete, and He is the head over all rule and authority;

Philippians 4:19
And my God will supply all your needs according to His riches in glory in Christ Jesus.

Isaiah 61:10
I will rejoice greatly in the Lord,
My soul will exult in my God;
For He has clothed me with garments of salvation,
He has wrapped me with a robe of righteousness,
As a bridegroom decks himself with a garland,
And as a bride adorns herself with her jewels.

Isaiah 54:5
"For your husband is your Maker,
Whose name is the Lord of hosts;
And your Redeemer is the Holy One of Israel,
Who is called the God of all the earth."

On whom are you depending to meet your needs and make you complete? If you have been expecting your husband to fulfill that responsibility, confess that to God and make a commitment to depend only upon Him for your fulfillment.

Look at your husband again. In your heart remove all those responsibilities and expectations you have placed on him that he was never meant to fulfill and humanly cannot fulfill. Now evaluate your relationship on the basis of God's simple plan.

Have you left your mother and father (emotionally as well as physically)?

Are you committed to sticking to the marriage?

Are you becoming one flesh?

If you are engaged, this might be a good time to note your expectations. Are they realistic?

If you are newly married, how are your expectations? Are you looking to God as your source or are you expecting to be made complete by your husband?

If you are single and feel that you are short-changed because you do not see a mate in you future, remember, you have the same opportunities as the woman who is married. God is your source and your resource. He is the Lover of your soul who never disappoints.

No matter what your situation, why not take a moment and write out a simple prayer asking God to deliver you from unrealistic expectations.

THE MYTH OF HAPPY LITTLE WOMEN

When you read the description of the little woman in *Moving Beyond the Myths: Hope and Encouragement for Women*, was it all too familiar? Refresh your mind by skimming chapter 6, if you need to.

Let's contrast the little woman with the description of the mature adult woman that God gives us in Proverbs. Ask God to help you honestly evaluate your maturity as a woman. It's time for your shorthand again, as you make notes to help clarify your thinking.

Proverbs 31:10–31
An excellent wife [woman], who can find?
For her worth is far above jewels.
The heart of her husband trusts in her,
And he will have no lack of gain.
She does him good and not evil

All the days of her life.
She looks for wool and flax
And works with her hands in delight.
She is like merchant ships;
She brings her food from afar.
She rises also while it is still night
And gives food to her household
And portions to her maidens.
She considers a field and buys it;
From her earnings she plants a vineyard.
She girds herself with strength
And makes her arms strong.
She senses that her gain is good;
Her lamp does not go out at night.
She stretches out her hands to the distaff,
And her hands grasp the spindle.
She extends her hand to the poor,
And she stretches out her hands to the needy.
She is not afraid of the snow for her household,
For all her household are clothed with scarlet.
She makes coverings for herself;
Her clothing is fine linen and purple.
Her husband is known in the gates,
When he sits among the elders of the land.
She makes linen garments and sells them,
And supplies belts to the tradesmen.
Strength and dignity are her clothing,
And she smiles at the future.
She opens her mouth in wisdom,
And the teaching of kindness is on her tongue.
She looks well to the ways of her household,

And does not eat the bread of idleness.

Her children rise up and bless her;

Her husband also, and he praises her, saying:

"Many daughters have done nobly,

But you excel them all."

Charm is deceitful and beauty is vain,

But a woman who fears the Lord, she shall be praised.

Give her the product of her hands,

And let her works praise her in the gates.

You may be thinking, That's great, but how do I become a mature and discerning adult woman? God, who is always sufficient, has provided a blueprint for success.

Proverbs 2:1–22

My son [daughter], if you will receive my words

And treasure my commandments within you,

Make your ear attentive to wisdom,

Incline your heart to understanding;

For if you cry for discernment,

Lift your voice for understanding;

If you seek her as silver

And search for her as for hidden treasures;
Then you will discern the fear of the Lord
And discover the knowledge of God.
For the Lord gives wisdom;
From His mouth come knowledge and understanding.
He stores up sound wisdom for the upright;
He is a shield to those who walk in integrity,
Guarding the paths of justice,
And He preserves the way of His godly ones.
Then you will discern righteousness and justice
And equity and every good course.
For wisdom will enter your heart
And knowledge will be pleasant to your soul;
Discretion will guard you,
Understanding will watch over you,
To deliver you from the way of evil,
From the man who speaks perverse things;
From those who leave the paths of uprightness
To walk in the ways of darkness;
Who delight in doing evil
And rejoice in the perversity of evil;
Whose paths are crooked,
And who are devious in their ways;
To deliver you from the strange woman [man],
From the adulteress [adulterer] who flatters with her [his] words;
That leaves the companion of her youth
And forgets the covenant of her God;
For her house sinks down to death
And her tracks lead to the dead;
None who go to her return again,
Nor do they reach the paths of life.

So you will walk in the way of good men
And keep to the paths of the righteous.
For the upright will live in the land
And the blameless will remain in it;
But the wicked will be cut off from the land
And the treacherous will be uprooted from it.

Meditate on the words you have read and write out a vision state-
ment for yourself. In three or four sentences try to describe the woman
you would like to be. If you really want to go for it, write it on a three
by five card and put it someplace where you will be reminded that
this is the "me" you want to become.

My goal is to be a wise, mature woman who . . .

CHAPTER SEVEN

THE MYTH OF DIVORCE IS THE END

Are you living in despair because you have believed the myth that divorce is the end? Are you struggling to overcome the pain and stigma of divorce? God knows and understands and provides comfort and healing. Let His words sink deep into your heart and bring peace to your soul.

Psalm 147:3
He heals the brokenhearted
And binds up their wounds.

Isaiah 43:2
"When you pass through the waters, I will be with you;
And through the rivers, they will not overflow you.

When you walk through the fire, you will not be scorched,
Nor will the flame burn you."

Romans 8:38–39
For I am convinced that neither death, nor life, nor angels, nor princi-
palities, nor things present, nor things to come, nor powers, nor height,
nor depth, nor any other created thing, will be able to separate us from
the love of God, which is in Christ Jesus our Lord.

Isaiah 41:10
"Do not fear, for I am with you;
Do not anxiously look about you, for I am your God.
I will strengthen you, surely I will help you,
Surely I will uphold you with My righteous right hand."

Psalm 9:9–10
The Lord also will be a stronghold for the oppressed,
A stronghold in times of trouble;
And those who know Your name will put their trust in You,
For You, O Lord, have not forsaken those who seek You.

Psalm 18:6
In my distress I called upon the Lord,
And cried to my God for help;

He heard my voice out of His temple,
And my cry for help before Him came into His ears.

This is a wonderful moment to stop and spend some time dealing with the Lord about the issue of divorce.

Maybe you have been judgmental toward your sisters who have gone through a divorce. If so, confess it. Ask God to give you His heart of compassion. Ask forgiveness of anyone you know you have hurt.

Maybe you have been less than concerned about God's heart on divorce. If so, confess it. Ask God to show you divorce through His eyes. Ask His forgiveness for not taking Him seriously.

Maybe you are divorced and have felt as if your life is over. Confess that to God and ask Him to show you His heart toward you.

Finally, maybe you have been the cause of a divorce in your own family or in someone else's house. If so, confess it. Ask God to forgive you, and if you haven't asked forgiveness of everyone you have hurt, do so. Then do what Jesus said. "Go and sin no more."

What has God shown you as you have spent this time with Him?

CHAPTER EIGHT

THE MYTH OF EVERYTHING IS AS IT SEEMS

L ife is what you make it.

The way you view your life is the biggest determinate of success.

It's not what happens to you that matters, but what you think about what happens to you.

As a man thinks, so he is.

What you think is determined by what you have been taught to think.

You are in control of your perceptions.

If all of this is true, it is urgent that we examine what we think and what we believe. It is critical that we filter the things we hear and the things we experience through the source of all truth. As you read the following Scriptures, turn them into a prayer. Allow God to examine the source of your thoughts and beliefs. If they are based on what you have always heard, what your culture has taught you, or what you have experienced, determine to replace that filter with the filter of God's Word.

Psalm 1:1–6
How blessed is the man who does not walk in the counsel of the wicked,
Nor stand in the path of sinners,
Nor sit in the seat of scoffers!
But his delight is in the law of the Lord,
And in His law he meditates day and night.
He will be like a tree firmly planted by streams of water,
Which yields its fruit in its season
And its leaf does not wither;
And in whatever he does, he prospers.
The wicked are not so,
But they are like chaff which the wind drives away.
Therefore the wicked will not stand in the judgment,
Nor sinners in the assembly of the righteous.
For the Lord knows the way of the righteous,
But the way of the wicked will perish.

Psalm 119:103–105
How sweet are Your words to my taste!
Yes, sweeter than honey to my mouth!
From Your precepts I get understanding;
Therefore I hate every false way.
Your word is a lamp to my feet
And a light to my path.

Psalm 119:133–134
Establish my footsteps in Your word,
And do not let any iniquity have dominion over me.

Redeem me from the oppression of man,
That I may keep Your precepts.

Joshua 1:8
"This book of the law shall not depart from your mouth, but you shall med-
itate on it day and night, so that you may be careful to do according to
all that is written in it; for then you will make your way prosperous, and
then you will have success."

Romans 12:2
And do not be conformed to this world, but be transformed by the renew-
ing of your mind, so that you may prove what the will of God is, that which
is good and acceptable and perfect.

John 1:14
And the Word became flesh, and dwelt among us, and we saw His glory,
glory as of the only begotten from the Father, full of grace and truth.

CHAPTER NINE

THE MYTH OF IT'S POSSIBLE TO PLAY WITH FIRE AND NOT BE BURNED

Consider the relationships in your life. Ask God to help you evaluate and see those relationships for what they really are.

Think of those relationships that are healthy, supportive, and uplifting. Think of those people who encourage and challenge you to grow in all areas of your life. Offer a prayer of thanksgiving for godly friends.

Proverbs 27:17
Iron sharpens iron,
So one man sharpens another.

Proverbs 27:9
Oil and perfume make the heart glad,
So a man's counsel is sweet to his friend.

Are you involved in a relationship that is demanding, controlling, unhealthy—a relationship that is tumultuous but you feel you can't leave because that person needs your help? Have you been successful in meeting this person's needs and changing his or her life? Or is this person becoming more possessive and consuming more and more of your time? Ask God to show you the truth about this relationship.

Proverbs 27:12
A prudent man sees evil and hides himself,
The naive proceed and pay the penalty.

Proverbs 13:20
He who walks with wise men will be wise,
But the companion of fools will suffer harm.

Proverbs 22:24–25
Do not associate with a man given to anger;
Or go with a hot-tempered man,
Or you will learn his ways
And find a snare for yourself.

Matthew 7:6
"Do not give what is holy to dogs, and do not throw your pearls before swine, or they will trample them under their feet, and turn and tear you to pieces."

Are you clinging to someone because you feel you need him and can't live without him? Has that person been able to meet your needs? Are you expecting that person to fulfill needs that only God can fulfill?

Exodus 20:3
"You shall have no other gods before Me."

Psalm 18:2
The Lord is my rock and my fortress and my deliverer,
My God, my rock, in whom I take refuge;
My shield and the horn of my salvation, my stronghold.

If you are involved in relationships that fall into the last two categories, ask God to show you how to resolve those relationships. Make a commitment to obey everything God tells you.

Proverbs 2:2–6
Make your ear attentive to wisdom,
Incline your heart to understanding;
For if you cry for discernment,
Lift your voice for understanding;
If you seek her as silver
And search for her as for hidden treasures;
Then you will discern the fear of the Lord
And discover the knowledge of God.
For the Lord gives wisdom;
From His mouth come knowledge and understanding.

CHAPTER TEN

THE MYTH OF LOVE

What is your expectation of love?

Is it based on good feelings and being sentimental?

Have you been disappointed as a result?

(Time for your shorthand, again, as you note what you have believed and what has happened as a result.)

Now look at your expectations and those disappointments through the eyes of true love, agape love. Evaluate them using God's description of love. Read each line of 1 Corinthians 13:4–7 and ask God to apply that truth to your understanding. (The definitions in brackets are taken from *Word Pictures in the New Testament* by A. T. Robertson; *The Expositor's Bible Commentary;* and *The Complete Word Study Dictionary: New Testament* by Spiros Zodhiates). Record the things the Lord reveals to you.

1 Corinthians 13:4–7
Love is patient [slow to become resentful]
love is kind and is not jealous [nor envious] ;
love does not brag and is not arrogant,
does not act unbecomingly [in an ugly, indecent manner];
it does not seek its own [interests],
is not provoked,
does not take into account [with a view to settling the account] a wrong
    suffered,
does not rejoice in unrighteousness,
but rejoices with the truth;
bears all things [does not delight in the faults of others],
believes all things [not gullible, but has faith in men],
hopes all things [does not despair],
endures all things [perseveres].

Remember that agape love involves commitment, action, desiring the other person's highest good, choosing what is best regardless of how you feel.

Ask God to show you ways to demonstrate your love. Doing what is best for those you love may not be easy. You may have to make some hard decisions. Trust God to show you what to do and to give you the courage to follow through.

Use your shorthand to write out what comes to your mind while you are reading the Word. Remember: the Holy Spirit doesn't shout, but He doesn't stutter either. If something comes to your mind, write it down. Test what you have heard against Scripture, and then ask God what He wants you to do with what you have heard.

1 John 3:18
Little children, let us not love with word or with tongue, but in deed and truth.

Philippians 1:9–11
And this I pray, that your love may abound still more and more in real knowledge and all discernment, so that you may approve the things that are excellent, in order to be sincere and blameless until the day of Christ; having been filled with the fruit of righteousness which comes through Jesus Christ, to the glory and praise of God.

2 John 1:6
And this is love, that we walk according to His commandments. This is the commandment, just as you have heard from the beginning, that you should walk in it.

1 Thessalonians 5:14–15
We urge you, brethren, admonish the unruly, encourage the fainthearted, help the weak, be patient with everyone. See that no one repays another with evil for evil, but always seek after that which is good for one another and for all people.

Romans 12:9
Let love be without hypocrisy. Abhor what is evil; cling to what is good.

CHAPTER ELEVEN

THE MYTH OF CHURCH IS ALWAYS A SAFE PLACE

What are your thoughts when you think of the word "church"?

What do you want from the church? What are you willing to give to the church?

Are you looking for a church that will minister to you and support you as you seek God's guidance in handling difficult situations in your life?

Is your church a place where hurting people (for the purpose of this book, women) can find support as they seek God's guidance?

The best way to evaluate how a church is responding or should be responding to hurting people is to look at how God responds to those people.

What does God use to mature His children?

2 Timothy 3:16–17
All Scripture is inspired by God and profitable for teaching, for reproof, for correction, for training in righteousness; so that the man of God may be adequate, equipped for every good work.

James 1:2–4
Consider it all joy, my brethren, when you encounter various trials, knowing that the testing of your faith produces endurance. And let endurance have its perfect result, so that you may be perfect and complete, lacking in nothing.

What plan does God have for service in His church? Is any person or group more important than any other?

1 Corinthians 12:7 (emphasis added)
*But to **each one** is given the manifestation of the Spirit for the common good.*

1 Corinthians 12:12–13
For even as the body is one and yet has many members, and all the members of the body, though they are many, are one body, so also is Christ. For by one Spirit we were all baptized into one body, whether Jews or Greeks, whether slaves or free, and we were all made to drink of one Spirit.

1 Peter 4:10 (emphasis added)
*As **each one** has received a special gift, employ it in serving one another as good stewards of the manifold grace of God.*

What value does God place on women in the church?

Romans 16:1–2
I commend to you our sister Phoebe, who is a servant of the church which is at Cenchrea; that you receive her in the Lord in a manner worthy of the saints, and that you help her in whatever matter she may have need of you; for she herself has also been a helper of many, and of myself as well.

Acts 9:36
Now in Joppa there was a disciple named Tabitha (which translated in Greek is called Dorcas); this woman was abounding with deeds of kindness and charity which she continually did.

How does God view the responsibility of all parties in a hurting situation? Does He give favor to one over the other?

Galatians 6:5
For each one will bear his own load.

Romans 14:12
So then each one of us will give an account of himself to God.

Are these traits present in your church? If not, ask God to show you what to do about it. Ask Him to make you a light not a scorching sun in your church.

Ask God to lead you to a church where His Word will be rightly divided and His mercy and grace will be extended to all who earnestly seek Him. He may show you that you already are there, but you haven't seen everything for what it is. Or, He may show you that you belong somewhere else. Either way, this is my prayer for you.

Colossians 1:9–12
For this reason also, since the day we heard of it, we have not ceased to pray for you and to ask that you may be filled with the knowledge of His will in all spiritual wisdom and understanding, so that you will walk in a manner worthy of the Lord, to please Him in all respects, bearing fruit in every good work and increasing in the knowledge of God; strengthened with all power, according to His glorious might, for the attaining of all steadfastness and patience; joyously giving thanks to the Father, who has qualified us to share in the inheritance of the saints in Light.

CHAPTER TWELVE

AND THE MYTHS GO ON . . .

B ut you just don't understand. My situation is different. I have
    tried everything and nothing has changed. The difficult peo-
    ple are still there. The circumstances are still the same. I'm just
stuck there. There is just no hope.

If your hope is in people and/or circumstances, then all is lost. That
is exactly what Satan wants you to believe.

So let's ask some nitty-gritty, rubber-meets-the-road kinds of questions that will help you determine where your hope is. Be painfully
honest with yourself. God already knows your heart so you can't im-
press Him. Then meditate on the Scriptures and record your thoughts.

Who is in control?

1 Chronicles 29:11–12
"Yours, O Lord, is the greatness and the power and the glory and the vic-
tory and the majesty, indeed everything that is in the heavens and the earth;
Yours is the dominion, O Lord, and You exalt Yourself as head over all.
Both riches and honor come from You, and You rule over all, and in Your
hand is power and might; and it lies in Your hand to make great and to
strengthen everyone."

If God is in control, why has He not changed the people and/or circumstances in my life?

James 1:12
Blessed is a man who perseveres under trial; for once he has been approved,
he will receive the crown of life which the Lord has promised to those who
love Him.

1 Peter 1:6–7
In this you greatly rejoice, even though now for a little while, if necessary,
you have been distressed by various trials, so that the proof of your faith,
being more precious than gold which is perishable, even though tested by
fire, may be found to result in praise and glory and honor at the revela-
tion of Jesus Christ.

"Where is it written" that God will always fix the people and/or circumstances in our lives? But what will He do?

Isaiah 41:10
"Do not fear, for I am with you;
Do not anxiously look about you, for I am your God.
I will strengthen you, surely I will help you,
Surely I will uphold you with My righteous right hand."

Isaiah 40:29–31
He gives strength to the weary,
And to him who lacks might He increases power.
Though youths grow weary and tired,
And vigorous young men stumble badly,
Yet those who wait for the Lord
Will gain new strength;
They will mount up with wings like eagles,
They will run and not get tired,
They will walk and not become weary.

When all seems hopeless, when you feel like a victim, what is your responsibility?

Proverbs 3:5–8
Trust in the Lord with all your heart
And do not lean on your own understanding.
In all your ways acknowledge Him,
And He will make your paths straight.
Do not be wise in your own eyes;

Fear the Lord and turn away from evil.
It will be healing to your body
And refreshment to your bones.

Do you believe that God is who He says He is and that He can to what He says He will do?

Do you believe it enough to give all the people, their opinions, and the circumstances you can't fix to Him? True belief brings about obedience. Saying "I believe" is one thing. Doing something about it is another!

You may have come to this point in fear and trembling, but you have come. Why not seal your commitment, no matter how wavering it might be, by writing it in a prayer to God. Sign it and date it. In the days ahead when you begin to doubt yourself and your decisions, go back to this prayer and ask God to stabilize you. Ask Him to remind you that you are free. Ask Him to keep you free as you walk in the truth that He shows to you.

Now to Him who is able to keep you from stumbling,
and to make you stand in the presence of His glory
blameless with great joy,
to the only God our Savior, through Jesus Christ our Lord,
be glory, majesty, dominion and authority,
before all time and now and forever. Amen.
Jude 24–25